A KURDISH FAMILY

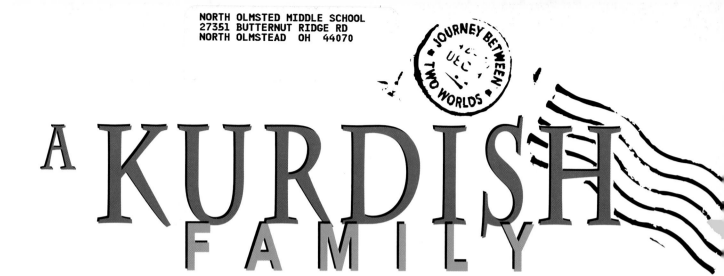

A KURDISH FAMILY

By Karen O'Connor

Lerner Publications Company • Minneapolis

The interviews for this book were conducted in the summer and fall of 1994 and in 1995.

This book is available in two editions:
Library binding by Lerner Publications Company
Soft cover by First Avenue Editions
241 First Avenue North
Minneapolis, MN 55401
ISBN: 0-8225-3402-9 (lib. bdg.)
ISBN: 0-8225-9743-8 (pbk.)

LIBRARY OF CONGRESS CATALOGING-IN-PUBLICATION DATA

O'Connor, Karen.
  A Kurdish Family / by Karen O'Connor.
    p. cm. — (Journey between two worlds)
  Includes index.
  Summary: Describes the experiences of one Kurdish family that was driven from their home in northern Iraq and moved to a new life in California.
    ISBN 0-8225-3402-9 (lib. bdg.: alk. paper)
  1. Kurdish American families—California—San Diego—Juvenile literature. 2. Refugees, Political—California—San Diego—Juvenile literature. 3. Refugees, Political—Kurdistan—Juvenile literature. 4. San Diego (Calif.)—Social life and customs—Juvenile literature. 5. Kurdish Americans—California—San Diego—Social life and customs—Juvenile literature. [1. Kurdish, Americans. 2. Refugees.] I. Title. II. Series.
F869.S22025   1996
305.891'590794985—dc20   95–33522

Manufactured in the United States of America
1 2 3 4 5 6 – JR – 01 00 99 98 97 96

AUTHOR'S NOTE

I wish to thank Mr. Taha Mohammed, his wife, Amina Ahmet, and their children, Khamger, Ferhat, Warvin, Zendon, and Susan, for opening their lives and their home to me.

I acknowledge their relatives and sponsors, Sakinah and Abdulla Barwari, for their kind help in translating Kurdish to English and for answering questions about life in Kurdistan. And I appreciate the help of Kurdish American friends Kaniah and Alan Zangana in locating and introducing me to the family. I also appreciate the cooperation of Cindi Britton, principal of Fuerte Elementary School, teachers Bruce Wollitz, Abdulhalim Mostafa, and Janan Hammi, as well as Russell Jaff, counselor to refugees at the San Diego office of Catholic Charities, for their gracious help, introductions, hospitality, and translating abilities as I put this book together.

And finally, my special gratitude to Ferhat and Khamger Ahmet, whose ability to speak English and to translate my questions into Kurdish for their parents provided a sturdy bridge between the family and me. My life is enriched for having met and talked with each of these generous people.

SERIES INTRODUCTION

 What they have left behind is sometimes a living nightmare of war and hunger that most Americans can hardly begin to imagine. As refugees set out to start a new life in another country, they are torn by many feelings. They may wish they didn't have to leave their homeland. They may fear giving up the only life they have ever known. Many may also feel excitement and hope as they struggle to build a better life in a new country.

People who move from one place to another are called migrants. Two types of migrants are immigrants and refugees. Immigrants choose to leave their homelands, usually to improve their standards of living. They may be leaving behind poverty, famine (hunger), or a failing economy. They may be pursuing a better job or reuniting with family members.

Refugees, on the other hand, often have no choice but to flee their homeland to protect their own personal safety. How could anyone be in so much danger?

Driven out of their villages by Iraqi soldiers in the late 1980s, many Kurds from northern Iraq fled to refugee camps in Turkey.

Although their school was bombed, these Kurdish children in northern Iraq continue their studies in the damaged building.

The government of his or her country is either unable or unwilling to protect its citizens from persecution, or cruel treatment. In many cases, the government is actually the cause of the persecution. Government leaders or another group within the country may be persecuting anyone of a certain race, religion, or ethnic background. Or they may persecute those who belong to a particular social group or who hold political opinions that are not accepted by the government.

From the 1950s through the mid-1970s, the number of refugees worldwide held steady at between 1.5 and 2.5 million. The number began to rise sharply in 1976. By the mid-1990s, it approached 20 million. These figures do not include people who are fleeing disasters such as famine (estimated to be at least 10 million). Nor do they include those who are forced to leave their homes but stay within their own countries (about 27 million).

As this rise in refugees and other migrants continues, countries that have long welcomed newcomers are beginning to close their doors. Some U.S. citizens question whether the United States should accept refugees when it cannot even meet the needs of all its own people. On the other hand, experts point out that the number of refugees is small—less than 20 percent of all migrants worldwide—so refugees really don't have a very big impact on the nation. Still others suggest that the tide of refugees could be slowed through greater efforts to address the problems that force people to flee. There are no easy answers in this ongoing debate.

This book is one in a series called *Journey Between Two Worlds*, which looks at the lives of refugee families—their difficulties and triumphs. Each book describes the journey of a family from their homeland to the United States and how they adjust to a new life in America while still preserving traditions from their homeland. The series makes no attempt to join the debate about refugees. Instead, *Journey Between Two Worlds* hopes to give readers a better understanding of the daily struggles and joys of a refugee family.

A Kurdish family crowds into a transport truck.

"I got four A's on my report card!" Nine-year-old Warvin Ahmet grins widely as he admits that he is especially good at spelling and math. He also enjoys learning new things, studying English, and making American friends. "And I like tetherball, basketball, and soccer," he adds as he pokes his head above the fence near his home in El Cajon, California.

But his apartment in this city east of San Diego has not always been home. Life in the United States is a new experience for Warvin and his family—father, Taha Mohammed, and mother, Amina Ahmet, brothers, Khamger (19), Ferhat (16), and Zendon (5), and baby sister, Susan (16 months).

Warvin Ahmet (facing page)
and his family came to the United
States in 1992.

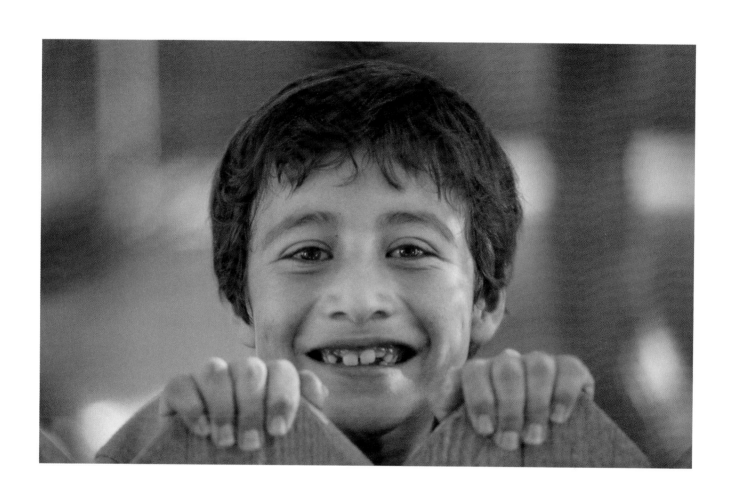

Warvin and his family are from Kurdistan, a mountainous region of the Middle East. Kurdistan, which has no official borders, extends over parts of Turkey, Iran, Iraq, Syria, and the former Soviet Union. In the heart of Kurdistan rise the Zagros Mountains, a rugged range that separates Iraq from Turkey to the northwest and from Iran to the northeast. In Iran the mountains gradually give way to a level highland called the Plateau of Iran. Rolling hills and the Mesopotamian Plain lie at the base of the Zagros in Iraq. West of this plain is dry desert land.

Kurdistan has deposits of copper, iron, and coal. The region's most valuable mineral is oil, which is transported by pipeline to major ports in the Middle East.

Some Kurds live in cities, but most Kurds are farmers. They raise sheep, goats, and cattle. In mountain valleys and foothills, farmers plant grains, tobacco, cotton, fruits, and vegetables.

Warvin and his family lived in a small village called Binaviah. Located near the town of Amadiya, Binaviah is in the northern part of Iraq known as Free Kurdistan. About 3 million Kurds live in Free Kurdistan. Kurds live in other parts of the world as well, including the Middle East, Europe, and North America. The worldwide population of Kurdish people is about 25 million. Most Kurds are Sunni Muslims, a branch of the religion of Islam. Their language is called Kurdish.

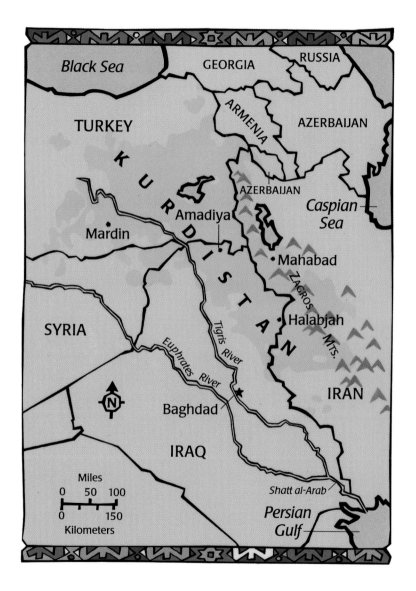

Thick forests blanket rugged mountains (facing page) *in parts of Kurdistan* (left), *a region in the Middle East. Warvin and his family lived in Binaviah, a small village near Amadiya in northern Iraq.*

Everyday activities—such as shopping at the local market (left)—have been disrupted by bombings in parts of Turkish Kurdistan. Damaged and vacant buildings (below) now line the streets of many Kurdish towns in Turkey.

Warvin and his family left their home in 1988, when Iraq's army attacked Binaviah as part of Iraq's long-standing war against Kurds. Ferhat recalls how Iraqi soldiers charged through their village early one morning. "We were eating breakfast when suddenly Iraqi soldiers ran through the streets shouting and throwing poison gas bombs everywhere. They set fire to shops and homes along the roads."

Thousands of Kurds had to leave or they would die. Young and old screamed and shouted as smoke and gas poured through streets and as fire raged through houses along village roads. Parents pulled children and pets from burning homes and fled to the nearest place of safety—usually an underground hiding place. They had no time to pack their belongings.

Warvin and his family hid in a big hole they had dug near their house. "Everyone had a hole like ours," remembers Ferhat. "When the bombs came, we crawled inside to hide from the soldiers. But the poison gas was so strong we couldn't stay there.

"My father said we had to leave the village right away. There was almost no time to get ready. We grabbed some blankets, a camera, a little food and clothing, and our horse. We had to move fast or we would be killed. We left our car behind. There were no buses in our village and no place to drive." The life the family had known ended suddenly.

Carrying all their belongings, a Kurdish family in Iran walks to a refugee camp.

Illustrated with flowers and vines, this verse is from the Koran, a book of sacred Islamic writings. The religion of Islam—which most Kurds follow—was founded by Muhammad in the A.D. 600s.

An ancient culture, Kurds are the largest group of people in the world without a country of their own. They have struggled throughout the centuries for their independence. But freedom has been hard to achieve because the Kurds have struggled among themselves, and the countries Kurdistan stretches across have been unwilling to grant Kurds their freedom. These nations do not want to give up rule of the oil-rich land and its people. As a result, Kurdish efforts to gain freedom have been harshly repressed.

For thousands of years, Kurds lived as nomads—people who move across their territory according to the season. In the A.D. 600s, most Kurds converted to Islam—a religion founded by a man named Muhammad.

During the 1500s, Kurds sided with a dynasty, or family of rulers, known as the Ottoman Turks. The dynasty gradually gained control of most of the Middle East (including Kurdistan) as well as large parts of Europe and North Africa. Together these lands were known as the Ottoman Empire.

As part of the empire, Kurdistan was divided into 15 regions called emirates. Each emirate was ruled by a Kurdish emir, who was chosen by the local Ottoman governor. But starting in the 1700s, the empire began to lose power. To keep their influence, the Ottomans took direct control in Kurdistan in the early 1800s.

In 1535 the Ottoman Turks seized Baghdad, a city in what is now Iraq. Much of the Middle East, including Kurdistan, was once part of the Ottoman Empire.

Kurds seeking independence for Kurdistan guard part of the region's border in the early 1900s.

They abolished the emirates to prevent the Kurds from gaining independence. A period of unrest followed, during which some Kurdish emirs and religious leaders tried unsuccessfully to overthrow the Ottomans.

World War I (1914–1918) led to the collapse of the Ottoman Empire. The war pitted the Allies (Britain, France, Russia, and the United States) against the Central Powers of Germany, Austria-Hungary, and the Ottoman Empire. After the Allies won the war, U.S. president Woodrow Wilson wrote a plan for a peace settlement. His plan stated that non-Turkish minority groups—including Kurds—who had been under Ottoman Turkish rule could seek independence.

In 1920 the Allies and the defeated Ottoman Empire divided up Ottoman territory under the Treaty of Sèvres. Like Wilson's plan, this treaty stated that the people of Kurdistan could seek independence if they wanted to. But the Treaty of Sèvres was never ratified, or approved. Instead Kurdistan was divided up among what are now Turkey, Iraq, Iran, and Syria. In the years after the war, Kurdish schools, religious groups, newspapers, language, and clothing were often banned in these countries.

When World War II ended in 1945, Kurds once again tried to gain independence. Kurds in Iran established a self-ruling region called the Mahabad Republic. But the republic lasted less than a year and was overthrown by Iranian troops in 1946.

In Iraq, Kurdish leader Mullah Mustafa Barzani and his supporters fought for independence from Iraqi rule throughout the 1960s. During this period, hundreds of Kurdish villages were destroyed and about 60,000 Kurds were killed or wounded. Hundreds of thousands of Kurds lost their homes.

To end the war, Iraq's rulers offered a peace agreement that allowed Iraqi Kurds more freedom than they had had before. But the agreement was never enforced, and the Kurds in Iraq renewed their struggle.

Mullah Mustafa Barzani led the Kurdish independence movement in Iraq in the 1960s.

The Iraqi Kurds received military support from Iran—a longtime enemy of Iraq. But in 1975, after Iran and Iraq settled disagreements over the border between the two countries, Iran withdrew its support of the Iraqi Kurds. The Iraqi military then rounded up thousands of Kurdish fighters and tortured and executed them. The military also forced Kurds out of villages near the Iranian and Turkish borders, moving families to towns and resettlement camps in the middle of Iraq's desert. Iraqi soldiers destroyed many Kurdish villages and more than 200,000 Kurds fled to Iran.

The war against Kurds in Iraq continued during the Iran-Iraq War of the 1980s. Iraq had invaded Iran, hoping to gain control of the important Shatt al-Arab waterway, which flows to the Persian Gulf and its bustling ports.

Kurds in Iraq sided with Iran. They hoped that Iran would overthrow Iraq's president, Saddam Hussein, who was strongly against Kurdish independence. During the Iran-Iraq War, Kurdish military strength grew. In 1987, to prevent Kurdish independence, Hussein gave complete control of important government offices in Iraqi Kurdistan to his cousin Ali Hassan al-Majid. That same year, the Iraqi army used chemical weapons to destroy a number of Kurdish villages. The following spring, the army dropped poison gas on the Kurdish town of Halabjah, killing at least 5,000 people.

Iraqi president Saddam Hussein opposes independence for Kurdistan.

Iraqi soldiers set fire to Kuwaiti oil wells as they retreated at the end of the Persian Gulf War in 1991. Soon after the war, Iraqi troops squelched an effort by Kurds to rise up against Saddam Hussein and his government.

In August 1988, immediately after the Iran-Iraq War ended, Hussein moved troops into Iraqi Kurdistan. The army began to destroy villages with poison gas bombs, often killing every man, woman, and child in the area. Thousands of Iraqi Kurds, including Warvin and his family, fled their homes and villages looking for safety in Turkey. Many left with only the clothes on their backs.

In August 1990, Iraq invaded neighboring Kuwait. Several months later, in January 1991, troops under the command of the United Nations (UN)—an international organization working for world peace—attacked

Helicopters (facing page) *transported many Iraqi Kurds to protected camps set up by the U.S. military after the Persian Gulf War. Other Iraqi Kurds traveled to refugee camps in Turkey* (above).

Iraq to try to force the country out of Kuwait. The brief conflict, known as the Persian Gulf War, ended in late February. A few days later, Kurds in Iraqi Kurdistan rose up against Hussein but were severely crushed by the Iraqi military. In April the UN demanded that Iraq stop repressing Kurds. To make sure Iraq's military would no longer attack Kurdish villages, French, British, and U.S. air force pilots began flying regular missions over northern Iraq.

With this peace, Kurds in Iraq were able to hold the first democratic elections in Kurdish history in May 1992. They formed a parliament, or governing body, in Iraqi Kurdistan. But life there is still difficult. International sanctions, or rules, established after the Persian Gulf War forbid countries from selling many everyday items to Iraq. And Saddam Hussein has halted the shipment of goods from southern Iraq to Iraqi Kurdistan. He also ordered all government workers—such as teachers and garbage collectors—to leave Iraqi Kurdistan. With few supplies, rebuilding is slow. Many Kurds spend their days standing in line for limited amounts of food and clothing. Many people go hungry.

Kurds throughout Kurdistan hope that one day they will have their own country. But without the support of the countries in which they live and without help from the United States and other democracies, Kurds know they may have to wait a long time for freedom.

When Warvin and his family fled their village in 1988, friends and family did not even have time to say good-bye. They did not know if they would see each other again or if they would even live through the days ahead. "Our life changed so much," says Ferhat.

Warvin and his friends and cousins did not know if they would ever play together again in the hills and villages. Amina wondered if she would ever go to the open market again to buy fresh fruits and vegetables and meat. She might never bake bread again or visit with other women of the village.

"We ran from village to village," Ferhat recalls, "trying to get away from the soldiers. But the poison was so strong we thought we would die. Every time a bomb fell, we ran to a stream for cover. We put our faces in the water to wash off the poison. Then we ran to another village and another." They hid behind buildings and trees and near the streams so the soldiers would not be able to see them.

"We kept on going for many hours until my father could get us to the Zagros Mountains," says Ferhat. Taha was a strong leader. "He knew the way over the mountains to Turkey because he had made the same trip many times before. He was a soldier in the Kurdish army when he was a young man. When he left the military, he became a salesman," continues Ferhat. "He traveled from Kurdistan to Turkey on foot to sell sheep, lambs, and other things. He was gone for many months each year."

Like Taha once did, this Kurdish man in Turkey brings his sheep to market (above). *Children play games in a small Kurdish village* (right).

A family sets up camp amid the ruins of a Kurdish town destroyed by Iraqi forces.

"My father knew a short way to go. It took us five days to walk. The other way was much longer. It was more than 300 miles (483 kilometers)."

Khamger remembers that he and his mother took turns carrying Khamlin, the baby of the family. She was only two years old and couldn't walk fast enough. "The mountain roads were packed with thousands of people and animals," says Ferhat. "They were all trying to escape, like us.

"Khamlin was also sick from the poison gas bombs. She couldn't breathe well. My mother was scared for her."

"All the Kurds helped each other," says Khamger. "We shared our food."

"We got milk from lambs and sheep that were roaming the mountainside," continues Ferhat. "We had a little food when we left home, but not enough to feed all of us for so long. For two days, we had nothing to eat."

At night the family stopped to sleep under a tree. Sometimes they built a small fire from scraps of wood and twigs they picked up along the footpaths. The family huddled together in blankets for a few hours before moving on the following day. "We didn't sleep well," remembers Khamger. They took turns watching out for soldiers and animals. "We slept and walked in the same clothes. And we didn't have enough blankets."

Tents cover the hillside of a crowded Kurdish refugee camp near the Iraq-Turkey border.

When the family arrived in Turkey, they were among thousands of other Kurds all looking for a safe place to stay. "President Bush from the United States sent American soldiers to help us," recalls Ferhat. "We couldn't have made it without them. They helped us find a refugee camp. They told the Turks they had to take us in."

"First we stayed in Camp Silopey, but it was not safe," says Khamger. "The leader of Turkey had made a deal with Saddam Hussein to get rid of the Kurds. So the guards treated us like prisoners. They didn't want the Kurds to get away and go back to Iraq. We didn't have enough food. Everyone got sick. They put poison in our water. They wanted the Kurds to die."

"After six months, American soldiers helped us move to Camp Mardin, near the city of Mardin in Turkey," says Ferhat.

Trucks (left) *transport Kurds to Camp Mardin in Turkey, a refugee camp where Warvin and his family* (facing page) *lived for almost four years.*

"It was the largest refugee camp of all," Taha points out.

"There were 17,000 people there," adds Khamger.

"It was so full of Kurdish refugees, the Turkish guards tried to get rid of some of us," recalls Ferhat. "And they did not want the American soldiers to help us. So they shot and killed American and British workers."

"They poisoned our bread and water," says Taha with anger in his eyes. "I have trouble remembering things now. I think it is from the poisoned water. My whole family lived in one small tent for four years. We were crowded and hungry, and we always needed more water than we got." Each day they had to walk at least one mile to get water from a well.

"I stood in line for water until 1:30 in the morning, even in the snow," remembers their mother, Amina.

"Only 10 people at a time were allowed to come and go from the camp," adds Ferhat. "We had to sign in and out whenever we wanted to go to a village to buy a few supplies or some extra food. The first year, we never left the camp. It felt like being in jail."

"When my father went to visit his sister in Iraq, he had to sneak out when the guards weren't looking," says Khamger. "He crawled under a fence at night to get away. I lied to the guards when they asked where my father was. I said he was in the tent because he was sick. They never checked. He was gone for 20 days."

When Taha returned, he and Khamger received money from a Kurdish leader in camp who gave each family money he received from the United States to help Kurdish refugees. With the money, father and son went to the nearby village and bought as many supplies as they could carry. Then they returned to camp and sold shoes and vegetables and rice to the refugee families.

Taha also earned six dollars a day by doing construction jobs in the camp. Sometimes he bought food with that money because there was never enough to eat.

"And the camp food was very bad," says Ferhat. "They would make a huge pot of soup," he says, holding his arms wide apart, "with only a few vegetables floating in it. They gave us meat once the first year. After that we got meat once a month and rice twice a month. Everyone got very thin.

"We wanted to be free, but we didn't know how to get away without being punished or killed. Then in 1989, a terrible thing happened. Our little sister Khamlin died," says Ferhat. "My father said her lungs stopped working because of the poison gas she had breathed in our village. And because we had no food when we went through the mountains. My mother cried every night after that. She still cries sometimes."

"Life in camp was very hard for everyone," recalls Taha. He waves his hand in the air and lowers his head as he remembers. "Bad food. Poisoned water. Soldiers hitting everyone for no reason. If you made even a little noise, or you laughed and the guards didn't like it,

The United Nations flew food to Kurdish refugee camps (right), *but people still struggled to feed their families* (above).

they hit us with a wooden board. Even children and toddlers. You could not believe all the bad things that happened in that camp," he continues.

Khamger talks about the women. Most of the time, they had nothing to do but cook and wash the family's few clothes. If the soldiers tried to hurt the women, their families would beat the soldiers away. The children had nothing to do either—no schools, no toys, and no books.

"Zendon was born in camp in 1990," says Ferhat. "His name means 'jail.' Camp was like jail for us."

Friends and family in the camp had to help Amina when she gave birth because good medical care was not available. "If you needed medicine, you didn't get the right kind," remarks Taha. "There was almost no help when someone got sick. If I said I had a headache, they would give me medicine for a stomachache. Some doctors gave people medicine even before they said what was wrong. The Turks made people suffer so much. There was not enough food, heat, or warm clothes. They didn't care. They wanted to be rid of us."

"And many people died for no reason," continues Ferhat. "Turks from nearby villages broke into camp and killed refugees while the guards stood and watched. They said they could not do anything to stop them. But they didn't try. The Turks hate Kurds. It has been this way for thousands of years."

Zendon—whose name means "jail"—was born in Camp Mardin.

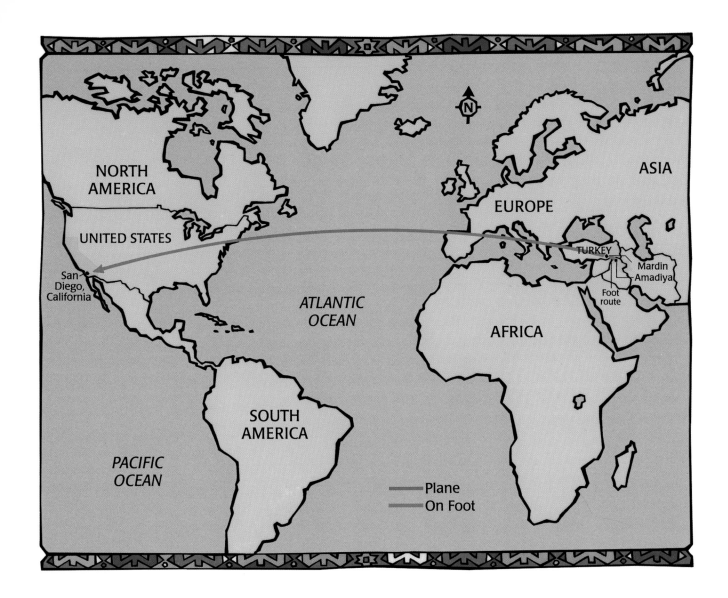

NORTH
AMERICA

UNITED STATES

San
Diego,
California

ATLANTIC
OCEAN

SOUTH
AMERICA

PACIFIC
OCEAN

EUROPE

ASIA

TURKEY

Mardin
Amadiya

Foot
route

AFRICA

Plane
On Foot

Taha's family hoped one day they would be free of this jail and could come to the United States. "But there were so many people who wanted to leave," notes Ferhat. "Not everyone could go. We were lucky. My mother's brother Abdulla sent a letter to the International Rescue Committee (IRC) in Turkey." The IRC is an organization that helps people escape a country where they are in danger. "He asked for our family to be released."

Abdulla Barwari and his wife, Sakinah, lived in the United States. They became sponsors, or people who help a refugee family settle in their new country. "We promised to help them get an apartment," says Abdulla. "We also drove them to their appointments and found schools for the kids. The IRC was very good," he observes. "They loaned Taha money for airplane tickets from Turkey to San Diego, California."

Taha looks at his pocket calendar. "On August 25, 1992, we flew to the United States."

"One month after we left, guards told some of our relatives in the camp that they had to go back to Kurdistan," continues Ferhat. "They did not have a sponsor. We got out just in time. Or we would have had to go to Kurdistan, too. We did not want to go back. After what happened to us, we would always be afraid. Life in Kurdistan is still difficult," says Ferhat. "I think our relatives are not doing very well."

The map on the facing page shows the family's journey from Iraq to California. Amina's brother Abdulla (above, with Susan) *helped the family settle in their new homeland.*

 Warvin prefers to talk about life in the United States, since he was too young during the years in camp to remember much. "My cousins Riving and Rawan and Rundik (the Barwaris' children) taught me to speak English when we came to America," says Warvin.

"They taught me, too!" adds Ferhat.

"But I taught myself to ride a bike," Warvin announces proudly. "The bike belongs to my new friend, who lives in our apartment building."

Ferhat and Taha talk about their first months in California. "We lived in Chula Vista with our uncle and aunt before we got our apartment in El Cajon," says Ferhat. "First we all lived together in their house, and then we got this place for our family."

"I like the United States," says Taha. "No one can do anything to you here. I was hit a lot while in the camp. The smallest thing would go wrong, and they would punish us. They took my money and tried to hurt my family and me.

"But it is also hard to live in the United States because I don't speak English. I want to learn. But it is not easy to go to school. We have only one car, and Khamger needs it for work. I cannot work right now because of the pain in my back."

Khamger explains that his father's injury is from a long time ago, but it got worse walking over the mountains to Turkey and living in the camps. "My children are learning English," says Taha. "They help me."

Warvin and his cousins (right) *have fun at a playground near his apartment building* (above).

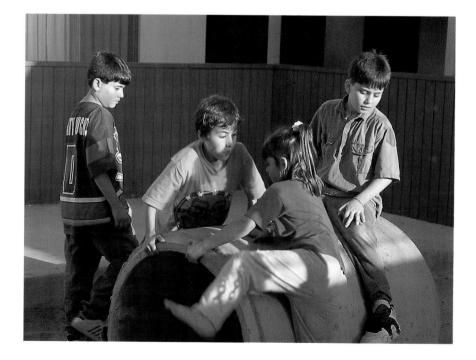

In the last few months, Taha and Amina also began studying English with a member of a volunteer group called Friends of the Kurds. Their teacher, Nancy, comes to their home every Tuesday evening.

Taha and Amina practice English and take care of their children and the apartment. Khamger works at Subway, a fast-food restaurant. Ferhat works at Burger King during the summer. "We give some of our money to our parents for food and bills," says Ferhat. "We also get money from the U.S. government. And this apartment is low rent for people who don't have enough income."

The eldest son, Khamger (above), remembers what life was like in the refugee camps. Taha plays with his young daughter, Susan (left), who was born in the United States.

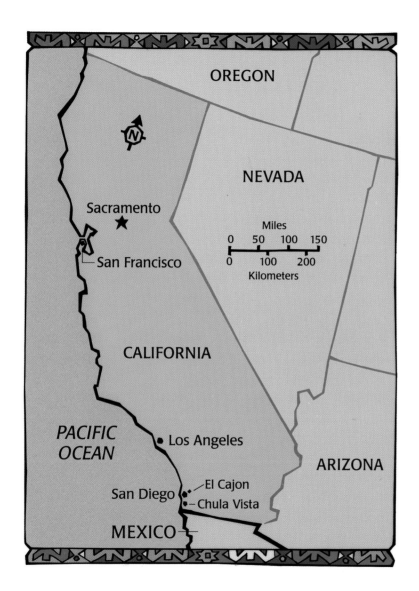

Taha and Amina settled their family in El Cajon, a city in the southwestern corner of California.

Amina likes the modern conveniences of the United States but still follows many of the customs of Kurdistan.

Amina looks on from the kitchen, where she is preparing dinner for family and friends. "I am lonely in the United States," she notes. "I miss my parents very much."

Her mother lives in Kurdistan, and her father is a refugee in Iran. He was a leader in the Kurdish military but had to flee in 1973 for his own safety. Amina, who was already married by that time, has not seen her father since then. Traveling to Iran was difficult and expensive. She felt she should stay home with her own family.

Amina looks sad for a moment as she remembers. "Everybody likes their parents," she says, "and I want to see mine."

Amina says her life and responsibilities in the United States are much the same as they were in Kurdistan. "Whatever women do, I do," she says. "I cook, clean, wash dishes, and take care of my family." But she admits household duties are easier in the United States. She has a kitchen with many modern conveniences. In Kurdistan she did not have a refrigerator or a stove or a microwave oven. In the United States, she uses all these appliances, and she smiles when she talks about how much easier it is to prepare meals. In Kurdistan she kept her food in bags under the cold water of a nearby stream and often cooked over an open fire.

Amina and her sister-in-law Sakinah (right) *prepare a feast of traditional Kurdish foods, including chicken with rice* (below).

But Amina still follows many of the customs from her homeland. Every Monday she squats on the floor of her small kitchen to mix flour and water and yeast into large balls. With her hands, she flattens the dough on a pan. She bakes the traditional Kurdish bread for a few minutes and then pops the loaves under the broiler until they are crispy around the edges. "It takes me the whole day," she says, wiping perspiration from her forehead. "I make many loaves and then freeze enough to last all week."

As Amina pulls warm, fresh loaves from the broiler, the family gathers and breaks off large pieces to munch on. This particular evening, Amina prepares a traditional Kurdish dish called *eprakh,* which is a mixture of

rice, meat, and vegetables. "I picked grape leaves from a farm," she says, smiling. "I dried them and put them in the freezer. Then I defrosted them and wrapped them around the meat and rice."

Amina receives some help in the kitchen as she serves the family. Her sister-in-law Sakinah prepares a salad of chopped tomatoes, onions, lettuce, cucumber, pickles, and salt. She scoops a large mound of white rice onto a platter.

"Come and eat," says Taha. He and Ferhat clear a place on the floor while Amina spreads a large plastic cloth for everyone to gather around. When the family is alone, they eat at the small kitchen table, but tonight there is not enough room for so many people.

Ferhat sets out plates and silverware (above) *as the family gathers for a festive meal* (left).

EPRAKH
(Stuffed Grape Leaves)

Eprakh is a traditional Kurdish dish. You can buy grape leaves in jars at many supermarkets and specialty stores. The leaves are packed in salt water and must be rinsed carefully before using. Ask an adult to help you with this recipe.

18–24 grape leaves
1 cup cooked ground beef
2 cups cooked rice
2 tablespoons tomato paste
1 clove minced garlic
2 tablespoons minced onion
¼ teaspoon salt
dash of pepper

1. Cook the rice according to the directions on the package and set aside.

2. Cook the ground beef in a frying pan over medium-high heat until brown, stirring to break the meat into small pieces.

3. Remove the meat from the heat. Drain off any fat.

4. In a large bowl, mix together the cooked rice, beef, tomato paste, and spices.

5. Drain grape leaves in a colander. Rinse the grape leaves in cold water. Dry on paper towels. Cut the stem off the leaves with a knife.

6. To stuff the leaves, place a grape leaf shiny-side down on a plate or countertop. Put a small spoonful of the rice-and-beef mixture in the center of the leaf.

7. Fold the stem end of the leaf over the filling.

8. Fold each side of the leaf, one at a time, over the filling.

9. Roll up the leaf from the stem end toward the tip of the leaf until you have formed a small roll. Gently squeeze the roll in the palm of your hand to seal the edges.

10. When you have used all the rice-and-beef mixture to fill the leaves, place the rolls seam-side down in a large saucepan or kettle. Arrange them in layers, if necessary.

11. Pour about a cup of water over the rolls, cover the pan, and gently steam until tender.

12. When the rolls are done, drain off liquid.

13. Serve the rolls hot or cold with lemon or lime wedges.

After dinner Warvin, Zendon, and their cousin Rundik page through a picture book (left), *while Ferhat shows a new science book to his mother* (below).

After dinner Sakinah offers traditional hot tea, sweetened with sugar and served in small glasses. "Sometimes with our tea, we eat *kade,* a rolled cookie made with sugar and walnuts," says Sakinah.

Later the women clear away the dishes and pick up the tablecloth. Someone turns on the television. Khamger says the family doesn't watch movies. They prefer documentaries and videos of Kurdish weddings and popular Kurdish singers.

Warvin and his cousins go to the bedrooms to play and read. Khamger talks about his plans for the future. "I want to be a lawyer some day," he says. "I couldn't finish school because of the camp, and now I am too old to go to high school in the United States.

"So I have to pass the GED (a general high-school equivalency test), and then I can go to [college and then to] law school." In his free time, Khamger enjoys playing the *bizuk*. This large guitarlike instrument often accompanies traditional Kurdish folk dances.

Ferhat is not planning his future yet. He is still learning English and going to high school. He looks at a science book he received as a gift. "This is great," he says, as he shares it with his mother. "Some of the words in the books at school are difficult for me. I have to study hard, especially science and history."

Taha relaxes on the sofa with a new book written in English. Ferhat leans over to explain the meaning of a word while Khamger reads one of his books. "Very good," says Taha. "I need to learn new words."

Khamger strums a bizuk, *an instrument traditionally played at Kurdish folk dances.*

 Taha and his family continue to practice their religion in the United States. Like most Kurds, they are Sunni Muslims. The religion of Islam is divided into two main groups—Sunni and Shia. Sunni Muslims believe that after the prophet Muhammad died, the spiritual leadership of Islam passed to caliphs (leaders) elected from Muhammad's tribe. Shiites, on the other hand, believe that only Ali (Muhammad's son-in-law) and his descendants are the rightful leaders of the faith.

"Our parents say the Islamic prayers, and sometimes they go to the mosque. A mosque is a little bit like a church. But it's far away, and they don't go often," says Khamger.

Although Khamger and Ferhat do not participate in their parents' religious practices, they do observe one Islamic religious tradition each year as a family. "It is called Ramadan," says Sakinah.

Kurdish Muslims pray at a mosque in Turkey. Taha and his family continue to practice the Islamic faith in the United States.

"Ramadan is a holy month of fasting and praying for forgiveness," adds Ferhat. "For 30 days, Muslims may not eat from morning until evening." At the end of the month, Muslims celebrate for three days. During the celebration, called Little Bairam (Festival of the Breaking of the Fast), they shop, cook, and visit with family and friends.

"The date of Ramadan changes each year," says Khamger.

"We also have Newroz," adds Ferhat, "the Kurdish New Year, on March 21st. We have a party to celebrate Kurdish history."

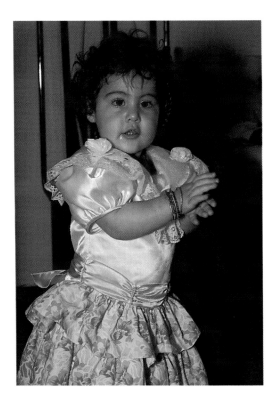

Susan was named after a flower that grows in Kurdistan.

Amina smiles at her children a lot. Tonight she sits with family and friends after dinner. She cuddles and kisses Susan, her youngest child, who was born in California. In the Kurdish language, Susan is the name of a flower. "It does not grow in the United States," says Amina. "But it is a very beautiful flower in Kurdistan."

After losing her daughter Khamlin, Amina is grateful to have her family around her and to have another daughter. She also likes knowing her family has a good place to live and plenty of food.

Warvin and his cousin Riving make funny faces.

After a long evening, the younger children are tired. Susan goes to sleep in a crib in her parents' room. Zendon sleeps on a futon mattress on the floor next to her.

Some nights they may listen to a story. "We don't have any folktales," says Ferhat, "but parents make up little stories sometimes, just for fun, to make their children smile. In camp our mother told stories about her family to help the younger children go to sleep and not be scared."

Warvin finishes playing with his cousins. He puts away his toys and books and gets ready for bed. He must go to school tomorrow.

Warvin watches Ferhat check over his homework before school.

 In the morning, Warvin's mother wakes him early. His father enjoys a cup of hot tea as Amina prepares eggs and Kurdish bread for breakfast.

"Time to go," says Amina, gently nudging Warvin to the door. Ferhat leaves first, then Warvin and his mother. They walk up the block and around the corner to the bus stop. Warvin and his friends go to Fuerte Elementary School, where Warvin is in fourth grade. "I like seeing my friends," he says, grabbing a seat next to one of his classmates.

At 8:30 A.M., the school bus pulls into the driveway of the school. "Mr. Wollitz is my first teacher," says Warvin, following a group of students into the classroom. Today is Warvin's turn to teach his science class about the human body. Then he watches and listens carefully as Mr. Wollitz holds up a mud puppy (a type of salamander). "They're used as bait to catch fish," says Mr. Wollitz. Next Warvin inspects the class telescope with a little help from his teacher.

"I learn English from Ms. Hammi," says Warvin as he goes to his next class. Warvin also receives help with English from a special education consultant named Mr. Mostafa, who speaks Kurdish and English. Warvin is happy to have someone in school who can speak both languages.

Warvin also likes tetherball. "I play when I come to school in the morning," he says, grabbing a ball and running to the field. "And we play at recess, too."

On the weekends, Warvin plays ball with his friends and cousins. "I like being with my family and friends," he says. "On Sunday we are all going to a park for a Kurdish picnic."

In science class, Mr. Wollitz shows Warvin and his classmates a mud puppy (left). *During recess Warvin likes to play tetherball* (above).

Once a month, Kurdish families in the San Diego area gather at a city park to share food, to dance, and to spend time together. Because Kurds do not always speak the same dialect of the Kurdish language, they sometimes have trouble understanding each other. But Taha speaks several dialects, so he can translate for other family members.

On Sunday afternoon, Warvin and his family arrive at Bonita Park. His mother and Aunt Sakinah have prepared a picnic lunch. But Warvin is not ready to eat yet. He runs off to play with his cousin Rundik and other Kurdish children.

At a Kurdish picnic, Amina prepares shish kebabs (above) *while Warvin and his cousins play* (right).

When Amina calls, "Come to eat!" everyone gathers around a blanket spread near a shade tree. After lunch there is time for volleyball and Kurdish folk dancing. "Some of the women are wearing Kurdish dresses," says Khamger, looking at the row of young women lined up to dance. "They look beautiful, don't they?"

Kurdish music is a big part of the family's life, especially at parties and picnics. The Kurds love to dance. They have many traditional dances that are performed in a line. Two or three people may start the line, and soon others join hands. Before long a huge line forms. People of all ages keep step to the beat of the bizuk. "Sometimes the men and women dance separately and sometimes we dance together," says Khamger.

Even children as young as three or four years of age try to follow along. "They begin dancing as soon as they want to," says Amina.

"The men are going to dance now," Khamger says. Then he, Ferhat, Taha, and other men form a line of their own. Someone puts on a tape of Kurdish music, and the men begin moving their hands and feet in and out. Soon they are laughing and singing along in Kurdish.

At the end of the day, Taha's sons carry everything back to the car. It is hard to say good-bye to family and friends. "But we will see each other again next month," says Ferhat, "maybe sooner."

Sakinah (third from the right) *joins other Kurdish women in a traditional dance.*

The Kurdish families also look forward to the International Friendship Festival held each year in El Cajon. The festival is only a few weeks away.

On the day of the festival, many Kurdish people dress in traditional clothes. The women wear long, brightly colored dresses called *kirasufistan*. Some, like Warvin's Aunt Sakinah, make their own dresses. Others buy fabric and take it to a dressmaker. Some of the men wear Kurdish suits known as *sheloshepk* and traditional Kurdish cloth shoes called *klash*.

At the festival, the Kurds share their culture with visitors. Kurdish families set up and decorate their booths, offering food and crafts.

In the late afternoon, Taha and Amina and their children arrive in traditional dress. They are ready to greet visitors and to enjoy a meal with their Kurdish and American friends.

"I'm going to the stream with Rundik," shouts Warvin. Susan, holding a big apple, runs after them.

"We like it here in America," says Ferhat, smiling.

"Our family is free in the United States," says Taha. "If you need help, you can get it," he adds, recalling that he and his family nearly lost their lives while living in their homeland.

"We like many things in San Diego. We can go to Tijuana in nearby Mexico," says Ferhat. "We like

Warvin and Rundik show off their Kurdish clothing at the International Friendship Festival in El Cajon.

A sign (below) *draws festival visitors to a Kurdish booth, where they can sample traditional dishes* (right) *and learn about Kurdish culture.*

picnics and going to the beach. I like the mountains and the trees. But I miss my cousins and friends in Kurdistan."

"And we like our apartment," says Amina.

Soon Warvin and his cousins return. Warvin takes a deep breath. His face is red. He is warm after so much running around. American tennis shoes poke out below his Kurdish pants. One shoelace drags on the ground.

"I like the United States," he says with a big smile on his face. There are no soldiers to be afraid of anymore. There is plenty of food, a safe place to live with his family, a school where he can learn, and friends and cousins to play with.

Warvin will always be a Kurd. But now he is an American, too!

PRONUNCIATION GUIDE

Ahmet, Amina (AH-meht, ah-MEE-nuh)
Barwari, Abdulla (bahr-WAHR-ee, ahb-DOO-luh)
Barwari, Sakinah (bahr-WAHR-ee, sah-KEE-nuh)
Barzani, Mullah Mustafa (bahr-ZAH-nee, MOO-luh, moos-TAH-fuh)
Binaviah (bih-nah-VEE-uh)
bizuk (bih-ZOOK)
El Cajon (ehl kuh-HOHN)
eprakh (ehp-RAHK)
Ferhat (FEHR-haht)
Hussein, Saddam (hoos-AYN, sah-DAHM)
Khamger (KAHM-gehr)
Khamlin (KAHM-lihn)
kirasufistan (kih-rah-SOO-fihs-tahn)
klash (KLAHSH)
Kurdistan (KUHRD-uh-stan)
Mohammed, Taha (moh-HAHM-muhd, TAH-hah)
Newroz (NOO-rohz)
Ottoman (AH-tuh-muhn)
Ramadan (RAH-muh-dahn)
Rawan (RAH-wahn)
Riving (RIH-vihng)
Rundik (RUHN-dihk)
sheloshepk (sheh-LAW-shehpk)
Warvin (WAHR-vihn)
Zagros (ZAH-grohs)
Zendon (ZEEN-dahn)

FURTHER READING

Bulloch, John, and Harvey Morris. *No Friends but the Mountains: The Tragic History of the Kurds.* London: Viking, 1991.

Francis, Susan. *Nowhere to Hide: A Mother's Ordeal in the Killing Fields of Iraq and Kurdistan.* Leicester, England: Ulverscroft, 1994.

Iraq in Pictures. Minneapolis: Lerner Publications Company, 1990.

Kahn, Margaret. *Children of the Jinn: In Search of the Kurds and Their Country.* New York: Seaview Books, 1980.

Kashi, Ed. *When the Borders Bleed: The Struggle of the Kurds.* New York: Pantheon Books, 1994.

Laird, Elizabeth. *Kiss the Dust.* New York: Dutton Children's Books, 1991.

Laizer, Sheri. *Into Kurdistan: Frontiers under Fire.* London, England, and Atlantic Highlands, New Jersey: Zed Books Ltd., 1991.

McDowall, David. *The Kurds: A Nation Denied.* London: Minority Rights Publications, 1992.

ABOUT THE AUTHOR

Karen O'Connor is the author of more than 30 books and hundreds of magazine articles on a wide variety of topics. Her children's books include *Homeless Children, San Diego, The Feather Book, Garbage,* and *Dan Thuy's New Life in America.* Her articles have appeared in *Reader's Digest, Seventeen,* and *The Writer.* An instructor for the Institute of Children's Literature, O'Connor has won several writing awards. She lives with her husband in San Diego, California.

PHOTO ACKNOWLEDGMENTS

Cover photographs by © Massimo Sciacca (left) and Rick Moncauskas (right). All inside photographs by Rick Moncauskas except the following: UN High Commissioner for Refugees/photo by A. Hollmann, pp. 6, 27, 30 (right and left); Sgt. John K. McDowell, U.S. Air Force, p. 7; © Ed Kashi, pp. 8, 9, 15, 25 (top), 26; Sarah Larson, p. 12; Laura Westlund, pp. 13, 32, 37; © Massimo Sciacca, pp. 14 (top), 45; © Peter Ford, pp. 14 (bottom), 25 (bottom); Cultural and Tourism Office of the Turkish Embassy, pp. 16, 17; UPI/Bettmann, pp. 18, 19; Archive Photos, p. 20; Department of Defense, p. 21; UN High Commissioner for Refugees/photo by Y. Sato, p. 22; Reuters/Bettmann, p. 23; UN High Commissioner for Refugees/photo by S. Berglund, p. 28; Textile cut-ins by Peter Ford